Worshiping the Sacramental Christ

Dennis J. Billy, C.Ss.R.

En Route Books and Media, LLC
Saint Louis, MO

Make the time

En Route Books and Media, LLC
5705 Rhodes Avenue
St. Louis, MO 63109

Contact us at
contactus@enroutebooksandmedia.com

Cover Credit: Sebastian Mahfood

Copyright 2024 Dennis J. Billy, C.Ss.R.

ISBN-13: 979-8-88870-235-2
Library of Congress Control Number: 2024946733

All rights reserved. No part of this book may be reproduced, stored in a retrieval system, or transmitted in any form, or by any means, electronic, mechanical, photocopying, or otherwise, without the prior written permission of the author.

For those searching for meaning in their lives.

"The Eucharist is the source
and summit of the Christian life."

Lumen Gentium, no.11

Table of Contents

Introduction 1

Chapter One: The Human Factor 5

Chapter Two: The Body at Prayer 23

Chapter Three: The Soul at Prayer 43

Chapter Four: The Spirit at Prayer 61

Chapter Five: The Community at Prayer 81

Conclusion: Sacrament of the New Creation 99

Introduction

The Eucharist, we are told, is "the source and summit of the Christian life."[1] This "Sacrament of Sacraments" immerses us in Christ's paschal mystery and is the means through which God both heals the world and transforms it. For this reason, it is also the "Sacrament of the New Creation." Jesus entered our world to divinize it with his presence. The change of our humble offering of bread and wine into the body, blood, soul, and divinity of Christ is the first fruit of this New Creation. Our Triune God is Creator, Redeemer, and Sanctifier. Although he always acts as one, each of the Divine Persons is typically associated with one of these three great divine actions: the Father, with the creation world; the Son, with its redemption; and the Spirit, with its sanctification. The Eucharist is the way by which this quiet transformation, this sharing in Christ's divinity, comes about.

This book explores the impact the Eucharist has on every dimension of our human makeup: the physical, the psychological, the spiritual, and the communal. As the "Sacrament of the New Creation," the

---

[1] Second Vatican Council, *Lumen gentium*, no. 11.

Eucharist touches every dimension of our being and transforms us into an organic member of Christ's Mystical Body. Chapter one, "The Human Factor," looks at Jesus' humanity and takes an anthropological approach to our celebration of the Mass. It points out the intimate connection between personal and liturgical prayer, shows how the Mass impacts every level of our human existence, and how each of these dimensions is intimately related. Chapter two, "The Body at Prayer," focuses on the physical dimension of our human makeup and demonstrates the many ways in which the Eucharist engages our five bodily senses of hearing, sight, hearing, smelling, taste, and touch. It views the material world as fundamentally good (yet fallen) and sees in the Eucharist our body's future resurrected existence. Chapter three, "The Soul at Prayer," looks at how our minds and hearts are nourished in the Eucharist, especially through the Liturgy of the Word when the Scriptures are read and broken open in the homily. It emphasizes the importance of reciting the readings with reverence and preaching in a way that touches both mind and heart. Chapter four, "The Spirit at Prayer," concentrates on the ways our spirits are nourished when at Eucharist. Silence is the language of God, and we must take some moments during the Mass to simply rest in silence and allow the Spirit to hover over the congregation and speak to our hearts. This is usually best done during the penitential rite, after the homily, or after the distribution of Communion. Chapter five, "The Community at Prayer," discusses the ways the entire Church worships during the celebration of the Eucharist. This involves not merely those present, but also all those who have gone before us marked with the sign of faith. The Mass is the worship of the Mystical Body of Christ and includes the Church militant, purgative, and triumphant. Each chapter ends with a series of reflection questions and a prayer to help us bring what we have learned before God. The book concludes with a summary of the various topics, especially about the Eucharist being the "Sacrament of the New Creation."

The purpose of this book is to alert us to the multidimensional aspects of our Eucharistic worship and to help us see how this sacrament engages the whole person and the entire People of God. It seeks to open our minds and hearts to the sacrament as the worship of the whole Church. It maintains that the human person is a microcosm of the Church and that the various dimensions of our human makeup that we find within ourselves are also present in Christ's Mystical Body—if only we have eyes to see and ears to hear.

Chapter One

The Human Factor

When we gather for Eucharist, we join Christ in his prayer to his heavenly Father. We do so not in an external, forensic manner, but in a way that unites us, as members of his Mystical Body, with his glorified humanity and enables our prayers to be one with his. When we receive the Body and Blood of Christ, Jesus, Our Incarnate Lord, who became one of us to redeem us through his sacrifice on Golgotha, we are immersed into the mystery of his passion, death, and resurrection so that our voices may ascend with his to the Father who created us and loves us beyond all telling. When at Eucharist, Jesus' prayer becomes our prayer, and our prayer, his. In this chapter, we will explore the anthropological roots of this Eucharistic action. We will look at how Jesus, who is fully human and fully divine, becomes our very food so that by sharing in his glorified humanity we might also share in his divinity.

Jesus' Humanity

Jesus received his physical being from Mary, his mother, who conceived him by the power of the Holy Spirit at the moment of the Annunciation (Lk 1:26-3). His soul was created by God and infused into his flesh at the moment of his conception. Mary's humanity, like our own, was physical, psychological (intellectual/emotional), spiritual, and social. Being immaculately conceived without original sin, however, she did not suffer from the unruly consequences of the sin of our first parents. These various dimensions of our human makeup are delineated by the Apostle Paul in his First Letter to the Thessalonians and in his First Letter to the Corinthians when he writes: "May the God of peace sanctify you entirely; and may your spirit and soul and body be kept sound and blameless at the coming of our Lord Jesus Christ" (1 Thes 5:23) and "For just as the body is one and has many members, and all the members of the body, though many, are one body, so it is with Christ" (1 Cor 12:12).[1] The Greek words for these

---

[1] All quotations from Scripture comes from *Holy Bible: New Revised Standard Version with Apocrypha* (New York: Oxford University press, 1989).

dimensions are *pneuma* (spirit), *psyche* (soul), *soma* (body), and *soma Christou* (body of Christ). The term *soma* (body), a neutral term, must be distinguished from *sarx* (flesh), which is a negative term referring to worldly allurements.

Because of the mystery of the Incarnation, Jesus' humanity contains each of the dimensions listed above. If in his divinity as the Eternal Word, he offers glory and praise to the Father with whom he is one, then in his glorified humanity he offers the same in a spiritual, psychological, physical, and communal manner that reflects the fullness of our humanity. "God became man," as St. Athanasius of Alexandria (c. 296-98 - 373) tells us, "so that man might become divine."[2] The purpose of the Incarnation, in other words, was that our humanity might be able to share in Jesus' divinity. This takes place at Baptism when we are immersed in the waters of Jesus' Paschal mystery, when we celebrate the other sacraments, and when we pray the Divine Office.

It happens especially at Eucharist, the "Sacrament of Sacraments," which is not only an action of Christ (like the other sacraments), but also a continuation of the Incarnation. In it, Jesus makes himself

---

[2] Athanasius of Alexandria, *De incarnatione*, 54.3.

fully present in the consecrated (and wholly transformed) bread and wine, and the sacrifice of Golgotha, when Jesus offered himself as a ransom for the sins of humanity and conquered Death through his resurrection on Easter morn, becomes present in an unbloody way. When we eat of the Body and Blood of our Lord, Jesus Christ, who is fully present, body, blood, soul, and divinity in the consecrated elements, we are united with him in a manner that reverses the digestion process. Rather than the bread and wine becoming a part of our flesh and blood, we become a part of Jesus' glorified humanity. And since Jesus' glorified humanity is intimately tied to his divinity by the hypostatic union that unites his human and divine natures, we also become sharers in his divinity. That is to say that, as members of Christ's Mystical Body, we share in Jesus' divinity just as he shares in our humanity.

Personal vs. Liturgical Prayer

Since in the Eucharist we become sharers in Jesus' glorified humanity, it follows that, as members of his Mystical Body, he prays in us not only when we celebrate Liturgy but also in our personal and nonliturgical communal prayer. He does so by his Spirit who dwells within us and cries out "Abba! Father!" (Rom 8:15). St. Alphonsus de Liguori (1696-1787) once wrote, "Paradise for God…is the heart of man."[3] God created us, and all of creation, so that he might befriend us, and we might befriend him. Jesus once said, "I do not call you servants any longer…but I have called you friends" (Jn 15:15).

According to St. Thomas Aquinas (1224/25-1274) and rooted in the thought of Aristotle's *Nichomachean Ethics*, there are three marks of friendship: benevolence, reciprocity, and mutual indwelling.[4] Jesus, in his mind, wishes us well and actively seeks our well-being, wants us to return his love, and desires to dwell within our hearts, while he yearns for us to dwell in his. That is what the Eucharist is all about. As "the source and summit of the Christian life,"[5] it is the primary means by which he seeks to befriend us. For this reason, it follows that everything we do

---

[3] Alphonsus de Liguori, *The Way to Converse Always and Familiarly with God*, chap. 1.

[4] See Thomas Aquinas, *Summa theologiae*, II-II, q. 23, a. 1, resp.; q. 24, a. 11, resp.; Paul J. Wadell, *Friendship and the Moral Life* (Notre Dame, IN: University of Notre Dame Press, 1989), 130-41.

[5] Second Vatican Council, *Lumen gentium*, no. 11.

begins and ends in it. When seen in this light, our devotional prayer (whether with others or alone) is oriented to the whole sacramental and liturgical life of the Church—and especially to the Eucharist.

Authentic prayer requires grace and, according to St. Alphonsus, "…the grace of prayer is given to everyone."[6] He also says, "He who prays is certainly saved. He who prays not is certainly damned,"[7] which is another way of saying that if you do not pray you will spend eternity trying to fill a big hole in your soul with all sorts of earthly, human treasures but which ultimately can only be filled by God. Such grace comes through us by virtue of our baptism and our reception of the sacraments. There is thus an intimate connection between our personal prayer and our participation in the sacramental life of the Church. Our personal life of prayer, in other words, flows from the prayer of the Mystical Body of Christ in its celebration of the sacraments—especially that of the Eucharist—and leads us back to it.

---

[6] Alphonsus de Liguori, *Prayer, the Great Means of Salvation* chap.2, conclusion.

[7] Alphonsus de Liguori, *Prayer, the Great Means of Salvation*, chap. 1, conclusion.

An Anthropological Approach to Prayer

From here, we can understand how the same human dimensions we use in our personal prayer are actually the same dimensions we use in our liturgical celebrations. This anthropological alignment coincides with the insight that the Mystical Body of Christ assumes the various aspects of human existence and then transforms them, eventually being all subsumed into Christ's glorified humanity. How is this so?

To begin with, we all need to worship God through our physical being (*soma*). Christianity asserts that our bodies are an integral part of who we are and that one day our bodies will be raised from the dead at Jesus' Second Coming. We can pray to God through our bodies in any number of ways: our posture at prayer, the gestures we offer to God when at prayer, fasting and almsgiving, the way we engage our senses and the world of God's Creation, taking a hike and recognizing the vestiges he has laid in his Creation, seeking to preserve his Creation for future generations by limiting the various ways we have been exploiters of the earth's resources—to name but a few. In the end, we need to find ways, appropriate to our situation in life, that will help us render worship to God through our physical being. That means that we must orient our bodies toward Christ in such a way that, created by God and kept in existence moment by moment, we offer glory and praise to him at all times in our daily lives.

We also need to render glory and praise to God through our souls (*psyche*), that is through our rational capacities (intellect, memory, will), as well as through our feelings, imagination, and emotions. In addition to our being physical beings, we are also psychological beings who possess an interior life capable of doing good (with God's help) but also of inflicting great harm. We need to orient this side of our human makeup to God through mental prayer, spiritual reading, creative writing, artistic endeavors, and sound friendships where we can share our feelings with others without fear of rejection. This dimension of our human makeup separates us from the rest of God's creation. With God's help, we are called to tame our passions so they may submit to the gentle rule of reason's reign to help us become fully integrated beings with the capacity to live, think, feel, and will all things for the greater glory of God.

Chapter One: The Human Factor

What is more, we need to be present to God in the spirit (*pneuma*). The spirit is the deepest dimension of our human makeup. It is that place within our hearts where the Spirit of God communes with us and cries out, "Abba! Father!" On this level, there is no need for words or bodily expression of whatever type. All we need to do is rest in silence for a few moments before the Tabernacle when in church or before a lighted candle or an icon of Jesus and Mary when in the solitude of our rooms. There is no need for words because the language of God is silence. He speaks to us in the quiet of our hearts. The challenge for us is to empty ourselves of all the noise and chatter that fills our minds, so we can rest in the divine silence that encompasses us. The Spirit calls us to contemplation, simply resting in the presence of God, to a place where we can be ourselves before him and allow him to dwell within us.

Finally, because there is a communal dimension to our human makeup, we are also called to relate to God in, with, and through others. We need to pray with others to become our deepest and truest selves. We can do so in any number of ways: by praying spontaneously with close friends, by singing hymns in local prayer groups, by participating in church processions, and by gathering with others in popular novena devotions—to name but a few. Because they are called the "domestic church" and the "church in miniature," families have a special obligation to foster a culture of prayer and reverence in the home. Grace before and after meals, praying the rosary together at designated times, blessing children before they go to bed, and attending Sunday Mass together, are just a few examples of how families can cultivate an atmosphere of prayer and devotion in their lives.

As human beings created in God's image and likeness, we are called to relate to God on every level of our human makeup: the physical, psychological, spiritual, and communal. When we do so, we relate to God as fully integrated human beings. When we fail to do so, we come up lacking in our prayer lives and in the way we relate to God, to others, and even to ourselves. Of course, there will always be a gap between where we are in our relationship with God and where we are meant to be. The key question each of us must ask ourselves is whether that gap is getting larger or smaller.

Chapter One: The Human Factor

Application to the Liturgy

Whenever we gather for Liturgy—be it Eucharist, the other sacraments, or the Divine Office—we do so as members of Christ's Mystical Body, the Church. Whenever we gather as the assembly of the faithful, our prayers are united with those of the faithful the world over, as well as with the Church purgative and the Church triumphant. What is more, our prayers make their way to the Father because they are united with Jesus' glorified humanity through the power of the Spirit that was unleashed upon the world on the day of Pentecost. Since Jesus took on our humanity, it follows that his prayer reflects the same four dimensions of our human makeup—the physical, psychological, spiritual, and communal—developed in the previous section. Furthermore, since the liturgy is the prayer of Christ, it too must reflect these same dimensions. And since the Eucharist is the prayer of Christ par excellence, it follows that, when celebrated well, it should also reflect them. How is this so?

The Physical. Whenever we gather for the Eucharist, we express our bodies (*soma*) in various ways. We genuflect, kneel, and cross ourselves. We lift our voices in songs of praise. We engage the senses with burning candles, incense, colorful vestments, stained glass windows, and statuary. We listen to beautiful music, process during communion, and receive the Body of Christ with our hands or on our tongues. We hold the chalice in our hands and receive from it the Precious Blood that is spilled for our salvation. These are but a few of the very many ways in which we offer our physical being to God in prayer. It is important to remember that Holy Communion means uniting our physical existence with that of Christ's glorified humanity. Since Christ acts in and through the members of his Mystical Body, it is important to remember that our actions in the Liturgy are those of Christ. It is through him, with him, and in him, in the unity of the Holy Spirit that we offer honor and glory to the Father

The Psychological. In addition to worshiping God through our bodies, we also offer him our minds and hearts (*psyche*). This takes place primarily during the Liturgy of the Word when the Scriptures are read, a Psalm is sung, and the Gospel is proclaimed. During the weekdays, the first reading is typically read by a lector and is taken from either the Old or New Testaments, which is followed by a Psalm, then the Gospel, which is proclaimed by a deacon or priest and is

Chapter One: The Human Factor

followed by a homily, which is also preached by a deacon or a priest. On Sundays, the same format is followed, the only difference being that there are typically two readings, one from the Old Testament, and the other from the New Testament. The aim of all this is to break open God's Word and allow it to touch our minds and hearts. The Psalms cover a wide range of feelings and emotions and should encourage us to get in touch with our own so that God's Word can shape not only the way we think and will but also how we feel. When done well, the homily should highlight the main themes of the readings and make relevant applications to our daily lives. The purpose of the homily is to shape us so that God's Spirit may be truly alive in us.

The Spiritual. When at Eucharist, we also worship God through the spirit (*pneuma*), the place where God's Spirit communes with us so that Christ may dwell in us and enable us to live as sons and daughters of the Father. God speaks to us through his Word but also in silence. For this reason, we need to find times during our celebration of Eucharist to simply rest in the quiet of our hearts and allow the Holy Spirit to work in us. When celebrated well, the priest will find times when he and the entire congregation soak in the surrounding silence and listen to the Spirit as he groans within our hearts and cries out to God with unutterable groans and yearnings. The time for this to happen is usually after the homily or after Communion before the final prayer and blessing. It is also appropriate to remain at our places after Mass and to thank God for the Holy communion of our hearts with his that has just taken place. During those times, the Spirit hovers over us and unites us with Christ's contemplation of the Father. At such times, we cry out with the Apostle Paul, "…it is no longer I who live, but it is Christ who lives in me" (Gal 2:20).

The Communal. Because we are social beings it is also important that we worship God together as the body of Christ (*soma Christou*). Christianity is not a private affair between an individual and God. While it is true that each of us can have an intimate friendship with God, it is more important that we look at the way we relate to others. Both Scripture (1 Jn 4:8) and the doctrine of the Trinity remind us that God is Love. Relationality, therefore, lies at the very heart of God's existence. Because we are created in his image and likeness, we, too, are relational beings. For this reason, we must worship together. As the Second

Vatican Council reminds us, we are the "People of God."[8] God saves us first as a people and then as individuals. He saves us as a people, his people, who are members of his Son's Mystical Body. That is why we need to gather for Mass each Sunday. When we celebrate the Eucharist together, we are proclaiming our faith in God and one another. We are saying that we not only belong to God but also to one another.

Finally, we must remember that these various dimensions of our human makeup do not act in isolation from one another but together as one, both in ourselves and Christ's Mystical Body. That is to say that, at Eucharist, Christ is praying to the Father through us, with us, and in us, just as we are praying through him, with him, and in him. Our bodily, psychological, spiritual, and communal dimensions, in other words, are united with that of Christ in a way that incorporates us into him yet allows us to retain our unique, individual personalities. At Eucharist, the Church is most herself—as are we.

---

[8] Second Vatican Council, *Lumen gentium*, chap. 2.

Conclusion

As with all Liturgy, the celebration of the Eucharist is a theandric action of both God and man. God has created us in his image and likeness with physical, psychological, spiritual, and communal dimensions to our makeup. When at Mass, each of these dimensions is united with those same dimensions of Christ's glorified humanity and offers glory, praise, and honor to the Father. Without Christ and the grace of his Spirit, we would not even be able to pray to God alone, let alone together. At Eucharist, Jesus unites our broken humanity to his glorified humanity, and we can share in his divinity and, with him, worship the Father in Spirit and Truth.

All this is possible because God created us *capax Dei* ("capable of God").[9] He did so because he wanted to enter into a personal relationship with his Creation, which means that he was *capax hominis* ("capable of man"). The sacraments are the concrete way that he has brought about this intimate friendship. As the "source and summit of the Christian life"[10] and as the "Sacrament of Sacraments," the Eucharist

---

[9] Augustine of Hippo, *De Trinitate* 14.8.11.

[10] Second Vatican Council, *Lumen gentium*, no. 11.

Chapter One: The Human Factor

is how this Holy Communion becomes a concrete reality.

As we have seen from St. Athanasius, "God became man so man might become divine." The Eucharist is the primary way by which this comes about. Whenever we gather around the table of the Lord and are immersed mysteriously the Christ's sacrifice on Golgotha, we become sharers in Christ's paschal mystery. That is to say that we live, die, and rise with Christ. The meaning of the word "Eucharist" is "Thanksgiving." We should gather for the Eucharist with grateful hearts for all that God has done for us by sending his Son to dwell among us.

Christ lives in us because he loves us, but also because he wishes us to bring his love to others. The Eucharist is one of the primary ways he does this.

Reflection Questions

- With which dimension of your human make-up do you feel most comfortable praying?
- Which do you find most difficult to engage?
- Which dimension do you think God is asking you to develop?

- Do you see a connection between your personal prayer life and liturgical prayer?
- Are the various dimensions of your human makeup considered when attending the Eucharist?

The Human Factor

> Dear Lord, help me to pray to you with every ounce of my being. Let me not hold anything back from you. I desire nothing but you. Help me to love you with all my heart, mind, soul, and strength, and to love my neighbor as myself. Help me, Lord, help me!

Chapter Two

The Body at Prayer

Our bodies are an integral part of our human makeup. We are not ghosts in a machine, but embodied souls created in the image and likeness of God. What we do to our bodies we do to our very selves. We are bound by a principle of natural law to preserve our health as best we can and, as the principle of totality tells us, to operate on them surgically only for our overall good. We are not free to do with our bodies as we please. We must love our bodies as we love ourselves. We must treat them with the dignity and respect they deserve because they are a part of God's creation. In this chapter, we will explore the various ways our bodies are involved when we worship God in the Divine Liturgy.

The Eucharistic Body

When we gather for Eucharist, we do so as the Body of Christ. We bring to this sacrificial offering our entire human makeup: physical, psychological, spiritual, and communal. During the celebration, we are united with Christ and immersed in his suffering, death, and resurrection. Our bodies play a significant role in this act of worship, if for no other reason than that our psychological, spiritual, and communal dimensions are expressed through them. Let us take a look at how the physical dimension of our human makeup takes part in the Eucharistic celebration. We will do so by looking at how we prepare for, participate in, and savor our celebration of the Mass.

1. Preparation before Mass. Before Mass begins, the Church asks us to prepare ourselves for receiving the Body and Blood of Christ by fasting for one full hour beforehand. This requirement tempered the more exacting demand of the three-hour fast that went before it, as well as the even more stringent requirement of not eating anything during the day before receiving Holy Communion. (This explains, by the way, why attending early Mass on Sundays or weekdays had become so prevalent in the pre-Vatican II Church). What is the reason behind this obligation to prepare our bodies to receive the Body of Christ? How can it be explained? Well, we refrain from food and drink (except water) out of respect for the Jesus' Body and Blood we are about to receive. In

Chapter Two: The Body at Prayer

doing so, we are affirming that the bread and wine we receive at Eucharist are more than mere bread and wine. It is a way of proclaiming our faith that the Body and Blood of Christ are heavenly food, different from what we normally consume, because they promise to unite us with Christ's glorified humanity, thus allowing us also to share in his divinity.

In addition to fasting, we need to arrive at Church sometime beforehand to prepare ourselves for what is about to happen. Although exceptions are sure to occur, it is a sign of disrespect to arrive late for the sacrament, especially if this becomes habitual. The same holds for leaving Mass early before the ceremony is complete. It is a privilege to attend Sunday Mass and a sign of disrespect to leave the Divine Banquet as soon as we can once we have fulfilled our Sunday obligation (e.g., after the moment of consecration, or after we receive Communion, or before the final hymn is sung). When, at the end of Mass, the priest or deacon dismisses us, he sends us out as a people to proclaim the Good News of salvation.

What is more, when we enter the church, it is customary to bless ourselves with holy water and make the Sign of the Cross over ourselves. We do so to remind us of our baptism when water was poured over our heads, "In the name of the Father, and of the Son, and the Holy Spirit." This simple gesture reminds us that we are adopted sons and daughters of God and that we are called to act as such. It reminds us also that we are called to be Jesus' disciples. As Jesus himself once said, "If any want to become my followers, let them deny themselves and take up their cross and follow me" (Mt 9:24). This simple sacramental sign affirms the unity of our human makeup, for it involves a physical action, a mental prayer, a spiritual reality, and an affirmation that we are entering the church, the physical building of which is a symbol of the assembly (*ekklesia*) of the faithful.

At the beginning of most Masses, only the priest, deacon, and servers normally process in. That is not to say that we, the faithful, do not participate in it. After signing ourselves with holy water upon entering the church, we should look upon our walking down the aisle and genuflecting or bowing before the tabernacle and taking our place in the pew as a participation in the procession at the start of Mass. For this reason, we should make our way to our places with reverence for the sacred space in which we find ourselves and in anticipation of the sacred mysteries of faith we are about to celebrate. We do so by silently genuflecting or bowing to demonstrate our reverence for what is about to take place. Once we have found our places, we either kneel or sit in silence to prepare ourselves for the beginning of Mass and the entrance of the priest, deacon, and servers. During this time, we stand as we lift our minds and hearts to God, thanking him for the gift of his Son and the redemption he has won for us through his paschal mystery and the sacred meal we are about to share. The word "Eucharist" means "Thanksgiving" and beckons us to celebrate Mass with grateful hearts.

2. The Celebration of Mass. The Mass usually begins with the ringing of bells and the recital of an entrance antiphon or the singing of a hymn. Thus, our senses are engaged at the very outset. The ringing of the bells reminds us that faith comes through hearing (Rom 10:17), while the recitation of the antiphon or the singing of a hymn highlights our call to proclaim what we believe (Mk 16:15). The ringing of the bells to begin Mass also conveys to us a sense that we are moving out of chronological (*Chronos*) and into sacred (*Kairos*) time.

As the Mass begins, we all stand as the priest, deacon, and servers process to the sanctuary either from the back of the church or from the side sacristy. This procession represents that of all God's People, and, for this reason, we are asked to join our hearts and minds with those in the procession. It is also an opportunity to remember how each of us processed individually before the start of Mass. After the priest and deacon genuflect before the tabernacle and reverence the altar, they go to the presider's chair and begin Mass with the Sign of the Cross and a greeting to all who have gathered, "The Lord be with you."[1] There then follows a penitential rite to remind us that the Eucharist is also a place where our venial sins can be forgiven (as opposed to mortal sins, which must be confessed in the Sacrament of Reconciliation). When we pray the Confiteor, we strike our breasts three times to signify our sorrow for even the slightest offenses against Our Lord. This physical gesture reminds us that even the slightest sin has repercussions on our whole being and that it is necessary to repent of our sins on every level of our human makeup, even the physical. On feast days and solemnities, the penitential rite is followed by the recitation or singing of the Gloria, a prayer that gives praise and

---

[1] All quotations of the Eucharistic Liturgy come from *The Roman Missal* (Magnificat, 2011).

glory to God our Creator. With extended hands, the priest then calls us to prayer and prayer the Collect (or Opening Prayer) on our behalf.

After these introductory rites, we sit in our pews and listen to the Liturgy of the Word. The Old Testament, Responsorial Psalm, and Epistle selections are read by a lector from the lectern, while the Gospel is proclaimed from the same place by the priest or deacon. The Psalm is often sung by a cantor. We sit during the First (and Second Reading in the case of a Sunday celebration) and stand for the Gospel, after which time we sit again to listen to the homily. All during this time, our bodies play a significant part in the celebration. We sit. We sing or recite. We stand. We sit again. We listen. This bodily movement reflects the movement that should be going on in our minds and hearts as we hear the Word of God and allow it to touch our hearts. This is also a reminder that the various dimensions of our human makeup are closely intertwined and cannot easily be separated from one another. After the homily, we sit in silence for a few moments to give us some time to reflect on what we have just heard and allow the Spirit to hover over us and rest within our hearts. We then stand to recite the Creed (if it is a Sunday or

Solemnity) and then bring to God our various needs and petitions to which we respond with one voice, "Lord, hear our prayer." This Universal Prayer of the Faithful reminds us that we can do nothing without God's help and that, as his sons and daughters, we can and should bring all our needs to him, understanding all the while that it is his will, and his will alone, that we seek.

After the Liturgy of the Word comes the Liturgy of the Eucharist. This begins with the preparation of the altar and is often followed by an offertory procession, where two or more of the congregants walk up the main aisle bearing the gifts of bread and wine that will be used to offer to the Father for their transformation into the Body of Blood of Jesus Christ. During this time, we can either sing an offertory hymn or sit in silence as the priest, deacon, and servers receive the gifts and bring them to the altar, where they are blessed and offered to God, the Father. After the preparations of the gifts, the priest prays a "Prayer Over the Offerings" that asks that this offering of bread and wine may be acceptable to God, Our Almighty Father. At this point, everyone participating in the Mass stands and the priest recites (or sings) the Preface, and continues with the Eucharistic Prayer,

Chapter Two: The Body at Prayer

which includes the Epiclesis, the Words of Consecration, the Memorial Acclamation, the Great Amen, the Our Father, the Sign of Peace, the Lamb of God. The distribution of Communion follows, either under one or both species. After those in the sanctuary have received, the faithful process to the front of the sanctuary (or designated places) as a pilgrim people to receive the Body and/or Blood of Our Lord, the former of which they can receive on the tongue or in the hand, and the latter of which they receive from the cup or under certain circumstances through intinction. A Communion hymn is often sung. After Communion, the faithful return to their seats and sit in silence, while the priest or deacon reserves the remaining hosts in the Tabernacle, consumes what remains of the consecrated wine at the altar, and cleanses the sacred vessels at a table set apart. After all this, another brief period of silence follows to reflect on what has just taken place and to allow the Spirit to move within our hearts. The Mass concludes when the priest recites the Prayer after Communion and blesses us with the Sign of the Cross. The priest or deacon then dismisses us, as they venerate the altar once more, genuflect or bow before the Tabernacle, and recess in silence as we sing a recessional hymn.

The point being made here is that we express our worship of God during Mass in various ways. We bless ourselves, genuflect, kneel, sit, stand, strike our breasts, listen, sing, recite, process, eat, and drink. That is not to mention the various other ways in which the celebration of the Mass engages our senses through beautiful artwork and statuary, colorful vestments, burning candles and incense—and the like. The sacramental nature of Catholic worship offers us many opportunities to orient the physical dimension of our human makeup to our Father in heaven.

3. After Mass. Once Mass is over, it is fitting for us to remain in our seats for a time to give thanks to God for the gift he has given us in the Eucharist. Whether we sit or kneel is a matter of personal inclination and does not matter. What does matter is that, before we go out into the world, we recollect ourselves by gathering our thoughts and making a specific intention to bring the Gospel to our family and friends, to those we work with, and to those we meet along the way. We should ask the Lord if there is any specific person we need to reach out to or if there is a specific task or work we should be involved in. Jesus' Spirit accompanies us at every step of our journey, and we need to be sensitive to his promptings. For this reason, it is especially important that, after Mass, we take those special moments when the Body and Blood of Our Lord are within us to ask the Lord for the grace to be open to those promptings. We know we are in tune with the Spirit when his manifold gifts and fruits become manifest in our lives.[2]

Christianity is not an introverted religion that remains locked within the self, but one that calls its adherents to go out into the world and make disciples of all nations (Mt 28:19). As Jesus' disciples, we are called to deny ourselves, pick up our cross daily, and follow him (Lk 9:24). Jesus wants us to be heralds of the Good News that the Son of God and has entered our world, lived among us, suffered, and died for us, and overcame the power of Death, which we inherited as a result of our first parents' original fall from grace at what the Catholic Church calls "original sin."

Jesus also told us that he would be with us until the end of the age (Mt 28:20). One way in which he

---

[2] See the *Catechism of the Catholic Church,* nos. 1832, 1845.

does this is through the gift of the Eucharist. Every time we celebrate this sacrament, he enters into our world, gives himself to us completely, and becomes nourishment for us, as well as a source of hope. For this reason, it is especially fitting that, as we receive his Body and Blood and contemplate his dwelling within us, we should be especially motivated to have him lead us throughout the days by bringing Christ to others. Jesus, in other words, wants us to follow him by being "other Christs." That is to say, he wants us the enter the various worlds of those around us, give ourselves to them completely by putting the interests of others first before our own, becoming nourishment for them by the support we give them, and, in doing so becoming a source of hope for them. The Eucharist is one of the primary ways he does this.

Through us, the Eucharist continues beyond the celebration of Mass and spills out into the world around us. Jesus, in other words, came not only to redeem us of our sins and transform us into adopted sons and daughters of the Father, but also to bring about a New Creation. He is the firstborn of this New Creation (Col 1:15), and the Eucharist is its sacrament in the sense that bread and wine, the work of human hands, are transformed into the body, blood, soul, and divinity of the Resurrected Lord. When seen in this light, the Eucharist is fundamentally oriented toward the transformation of the world around us. It does not end with the conclusion of Mass but, through Christ living in us, spills out into the Liturgy of the World and is celebrated by the Mystical Body, the Church, with Christ as its head and its members. What does this mean concretely?

To begin with, it does not mean that the Mass itself does not have boundaries with a clear beginning, middle, and end. The Liturgies of the Word and Eucharist are distinct in and of themselves and, together, form one of the seven sacraments of the Church, which is the sacrament of Christ, as Christ is the sacrament of God. What it *does* mean, however, is that the eschatological, already-but-not-yet, character of the sacrament affects not only those attending the sacrament itself but also the world at large, indeed, the entire universe. There is a cosmic dimension to the Eucharist at work in the world. When we celebrate this sacrament, we anticipate the transformation not only of ourselves but also of the entire universe. God, in other words, exists not outside the universe, but the universe exists in God while remaining distinct from him as a part of his creation.

Whenever we say, "Maranatha, Come Lord Jesus" (1 Cor 16:22), we affirm Jesus' coming at the end of time when the final transformation of our world into the New Creation will come about.

The Priesthood of the Faithful

One way of understanding the Eucharist both during Mass and after it, is to look at the relationship between the ordained ministerial priesthood and the priesthood of the laity. According to Catholic belief, there is not only the priesthood of Christ, but also various degrees of participation. The highest grade of participation in Christ's priesthood lies in the episcopacy and varying other degrees in the presbyterate and the diaconate. These three levels of the ordained ministerial priesthood involve an ontological change (different from the character or seal they received in baptism) in the ordinands and confer on them the ability to administer the sacraments. Bishops can administer all seven sacraments. Priests can administer five—baptism, reconciliation, Eucharist, marriage, and the anointing of the sick—and can also be delegated by their local bishop to administer confirmation. Deacons, in turn, can administer baptism and the sacrament of matrimony.

By virtue of their baptism, the laity also share in Christ's priesthood in a real, yet nonetheless lesser, degree. They can baptize in emergencies when no priest or deacon is available and they bring the Gospel to the world, especially to their families, the workplace, and the community at large. They do this in a way that those in the administerial priesthood cannot. They bring the body of Christ to nursing homes and hospitals, to ghettos and farmlands, to hotels and prisons, to peace talks and battlefields, to cruise ships and prisons, to corporate headquarters and factories, to the rich and the homeless, to young and to old, to the sick and dying, to the living and the dead. Wherever the laity goes, they are called to bring Christ to others, not in its sacramental form, but in a lesser, yet real, degree.

The priesthood of Christ includes the offices (or *munera*) of priest, prophet, and king. Although the laity carries out these offices in different degrees from the ordained priesthood, they do so in a way that is essential to the spread of the Gospel. By their priestly sharing in the one priesthood of Christ, the laity are called to extend the Mass in an eschatological (already-but not-yet) manner once the sacrament itself has ended. In other words, they are called to be Eucharist for others, and they are called to do so in the threefold way of banquet, sacrifice, and presence. That is to say that, pointing to the messianic banquet, they act in ways to become nourishment for others; pointing to the sacrifice of Christ on the cross in which they were immersed at Mass, they give themselves to others in selfless ways; and pointing to Christ's presence in the consecrated bread and wine, they bring the presence of Christ to others by the friendship they share with him. When the laity leave Mass, they bless themselves with holy water, just as they did when they first entered the church. This simple sacramental action signifies the continuity between the sacrament confected at Mass and its eschatological continuation afterward. The laity play a significant role in this Eucharistic continuation. When seen in this light, the words of the priest, "Go forth! The Mass is ended," takes on an even deeper meaning.

Conclusion

When we gather to celebrate the Eucharist, we are called to give honor and glory to God on every level of our human makeup. Our bodies are an essential part of that makeup and this needs to be intentionally oriented toward God in ways that include all aspects of our physical existence. We need to engage all the senses: our hearing, sight, touch, smell, and taste. We need to use voice and song, gesture and posture, motion and stillness. We need to sit and listen, sing and dance, eat and drink. If we fail to do so, we are holding something back and not worshiping God on every level of our human makeup.

In this chapter, we have seen the various ways in our Eucharistic celebrations that we use our bodies to render thanks to God for the gift he has given us in his Son's paschal mystery. Jesus' resurrection from the dead gives us hope that we, too, will one day rise again and through him enter into the presence of his heavenly Father. It also tells us that the physical dimension of our lives will not simply decay and return to the dust from which it came but will one day rise from its tomb and be transformed to share in Christ's glorified humanity. Such a sharing is itself eschatological since it is already here but will come to fruition in the life that awaits us.

Finally, we have also seen that, although the sacramental celebration of the Eucharist ends when the priest or deacon dismisses the congregation, its eschatological (already-but-not-yet) dimension continues beyond the walls of the church and that the laity, by their sharing in the one priesthood of Christ (albeit in a lesser degree), play an important role in this continuance. The laity are called to bring Christ to the world in ways that the ordained, ministerial priesthood simply cannot. As members of the Mystical Body of Christ, they share in the kingly, priestly, and prophetic offices of Christ. They, too, are called to make disciples of all nations. They do so by remaining faithful to their noble vocation. When seen in this light, with dismissal by the priest or deacon, their work has only just begun.

Reflection Questions

- In what ways are you physically engaged when you attend the Eucharist?
- Which of these do you enjoy the most?

Chapter Two: The Body at Prayer 41

- Which of these helps you to give glory and honor and praise to God?
- Is there anything you think that should be toned down?
- How could your Sunday worship be improved?

The Body at Prayer

Lord, the soul is willing, but the flesh is weak. Help me to place my body under the gentle reign of your Spirit. Help me to offer you my material existence in a continual sacrifice of glory, praise and thanksgiving. Help me take care of my body so I may continue to offer you glory and praise for years on end.

Chapter Three

The Soul at Prayer

There are many dimensions to our human makeup. We are more than just physical beings. We also have psychological beings with the capacity to think, will, remember, imagine, and feel. In this chapter, we will examine this aspect of our existence and see how we are called to orient every aspect of the soul (*psyche* in Greek) to the Lord during our Eucharistic celebrations. Although we always act as one, different aspects of our human makeup come to the fore depending on the particular activity we are engaged in. The same holds for our liturgical celebrations. If there is a time and season for everything under the sun, then, at Eucharist, there are times specifically dedicated to the nourishment of our souls.

What Is Soul (Psyche)?

What exactly do we mean by soul? How can we describe it? How can we recognize its elusive character? Of what is it comprised? To what extent does it animate and make us whole? The soul (*psyche*) is an important aspect of our human makeup. Without it, we would not be who we are. We would not be created in the image and likeness of God. The human soul stands for the rational part of who we are. We have reason, which gives us the ability to think and reflect on our lives. We also have a rational appetite known as the will, which enables us to direct our actions toward specific ends. We have internal senses such as memory and imagination, which help us make the past present and face the future with a wide range of possibilities. We also have our five external senses of sight, hearing, taste, touch, and smell, all of which enable us to interact with the external world. The human soul (*psyche*) animates our bodies and gives them shape. Human beings are a composite of body and soul. The body without the soul is nothing but a lifeless material mass. The soul without the body is an immortal but incomplete human entity since it exists to enliven the body and, without it, fails to reach its fullest potential. Let us look at the various dimensions of the human *psyche*. Doing so will help us understand its role in divine worship.

To begin with, it is important to point out that "soul" is an analogous concept. The soul of a plant is different from that of an animal or a human being. All three are similar yet different. They animate and bring life to whatever bodies they inhabit but in different ways. What is more, our rational souls are of a higher nature and can incorporate into themselves the various properties of animal and vegetative souls. That is to say that, in addition to our capacity to think rationally and will objects of our own choice, we can access the outer world through our five senses (as animals do) and be nourished by water and the riches of the soil (as do plants). At the dawn of Creation, all the senses and properties of the animal and vegetative soul were in sync with our rational powers and governed by the gentle rule of reason's reign. Our internal senses of memory and imagination also cooperated with this sovereign rule. The will (or rational appetite), moreover, was oriented toward the good presented to it by reason, and reason itself was in tune with Eternal Reason. Every aspect of our soul lived in harmony and peace. We were in harmony with ourselves, others, and all of creation.

However, after our first parents' fall from grace, the lower animal and vegetative powers of the human soul became unruly and no longer responded to reason's rule. What is more, reason itself became darkened and will (our rational appetite) weakened. Our internal senses of memory and imagination also became unruly, while our feelings and emotions rebelled against our soul's higher powers. Created in the image and likeness of God, we remained ontologically good, but we were corrupted and could easily be led astray by the lure of the world and the desire for power, pleasure, and possessions. Because of this weakened condition, we gradually sank into our animal senses and tended to lead vicious lives rather than lives of virtue. Jesus came to heal us of these deep, self-inflicted wounds. He embraced the cross and conquered death not merely to restore to us what we had lost but to elevate us to even higher levels. The Eucharist is the primary means by which we enter into contact with this transforming power.

The Soul at Prayer

Although there are many dimensions of our human makeup, we are integrated beings and always act as one. From this, it follows that the various dimensions of our lives—the physical, psychological, spiritual, and communal—always act as an integrated whole. Depending on the activity, however, one of these dimensions may come to the fore and even be dominant. For example, the various activities

Chapter Three: The Soul at Prayer

outlined in the previous chapter that engage the body do not exclude the psychological, spiritual, or communal sides of our nature from participating in the action. They, too, are involved in the action, although perhaps with less intensity. In this section, we will look at those actions during our celebration of the Eucharist when the psychological/intellectual side of us is especially involved. Although this side of us is always involved in our celebrations, there are times when it is particularly engaged.

The Penitential Rite is one such case. After the opening greeting, the priest invites us to examine our minds and hearts and asks God to forgive us our sins. At this time, we should pause and examine our conscience to get in touch with the various ways in which we have offended God, others, and even ourselves. We do this as individuals but also as a believing community. The words we pray together, be it the Confiteor or the "Lord have mercy," must come from the heart and express our deep sorrow for the way we have offended God and those around us. If we do not take this time to examine ourselves and get in touch with our offense against God and neighbor, then the words we say, whatever they may be, become nothing but empty sounds uttered without force or meaning.

When we *do* say them sincerely with both mind and heart, they become grace-filled, healing, and transformative signs of true contrition.

Another time when our minds and hearts are particularly engaged comes at the Liturgy of the Word. During the First Reading, the singing of the Responsorial Psalm, the Second Reading (if there is one), and the proclamation of the Gospel, we are called to listen attentively to what is being said. The art of active listening is a skill that needs to be intentionally taught and learned. During this time, we are called to give focused attention to the lectors, cantor, and especially the deacon or priest as God's Word is announced to those present. God is always speaking to us when his Word is proclaimed, but we need to be able to listen to what he is saying to us. Our responses, "Thanks be to God" (after the first and second readings) and "Praise to you, Lord Jesus Christ" (after the proclamation of the Gospel), should also be expressed with deep conviction and gratitude for the gift of God's Word to us. It goes without saying that we should give our full attention to the homily given by the priest or deacon. Rather than criticizing the style of delivery or even the points being made, we should listen with care and look for something to

Chapter Three: The Soul at Prayer

take away from us that will help us on our spiritual journey. Regardless of the quality of the homily itself, God still speaks to us through the proclamation of the Word. We should not be passive onlookers during the celebration of the Liturgy of the Word but active participants seeking to find that one pearl of wisdom to take away with us as we go on with the day. After the homily, we should rest in silence for a few moments to allow what we have heard to penetrate our minds and hearts and touch our spirits. Then, when we conclude the Liturgy of the Word with the Prayer of the Faithful, we should listen to the various needs and petitions we are giving to God and bring to him our own needs and wants either in word or in the quiet of our hearts. The Liturgy of the Word is one of the most important times during our celebration of the Eucharist when the psychological dimension of our human makeup (our minds and hearts) is engaged, nourished, and even challenged.

The Offertory Procession and Preparation of the Gifts are yet other times when our minds and hearts are engaged during our celebration Eucharist. The Procession represents our spiritual journey throughout life when we present to the priest the work of our hands and offer it up to God as a sign of gratitude for all he has done for us in sending his Son to die for us and liberate us from sin and Death's stranglehold over us. During that time, we are asked to imagine ourselves journeying with those bearing the gifts of bread and wine. That journey lasts a lifetime and is something that, for most of us, continues after death until we become ready to come face-to-face with the Lord. This exercise of the imagination represents a further participation of our soul (*psyche*) in the celebration. The bread and wine, which will soon be transformed into the body, blood, soul, and divinity of Christ, point to the transformation that we will one day undergo in the resurrection. This process of divinization is already taking place through our participation in the Church's Eucharistic worship. When we eat and drink the body and blood of God's Son, what we receive is gradually and gently over time making us other christs. The Eucharist, in other words, is God's chosen way to help us share in his divinity. After all, he created us in his image and likeness so that we might become like him. Although God always acts as one, each Person in the Blessed Trinity is typically associated with one of the acts of the Divine Economy: the Father with Creation; the Son with Redemption; and the Spirit with Sancti-

Chapter Three: The Soul at Prayer

fication. When we celebrate the Eucharist, all three of these actions take place simultaneously: The Father continues to create us and keep us in being; the Son makes present his sacrificial act of redemption and applies it to our own lives; the Spirit sanctifies us and makes us holy. When the priest offers our gifts to the Father, he does so in the Spirit and we, looking at this sacrificial offering through the eyes of faith, are united with him in the Spirit as his Mystical Body.

The Liturgy of the Eucharist, which begins with the Offering of the Gifts and continues with the Preface of the Mass and the Eucharistic Prayer, and which culminates with the Memorial Acclamation and the Great Amen, involves us in a great act of remembering. Someone once said, "Something is not fully experienced until it is remembered." This part of the Mass engages every aspect of the soul, but especially the internal sense of memory. By remembering Jesus' parting meal with his disciples, we experience it anew. And since Jesus' Last Supper is intimately linked to his death on Golgotha, this great act of remembering also immerses us in his Paschal Mystery, which ultimately leads to the empty tomb of Easter Morning. The epiclesis part of the Eucharist Prayer asks God to send down his Spirit upon the humble gifts of bread and wine we are offering him so they may become the Body and Blood of Our Lord, Jesus Christ, and puts this great act of remembering in its proper perspective. It immerses us in Jesus' passion, death, and resurrection, is an act of Christ's Mystical Body, the Church, and requires the grace of the Spirit since it presupposes the theological virtues of faith, hope, and love, all of which require God's grace. This great act of remembering, therefore, has both objective and subjective qualities. On the one hand, the Spirit descends upon the offerings to transform them into Christ's body and blood. On the other hand, this mysterious change can only be perceived through the eyes of faith, which allows us to perceive something beyond what the empirical world can verify. After the priest, acting in the person of Christ (*in persona Christi*) recites the words of consecration, this transformation takes place and the entire believing community proclaims the mystery of faith and is later followed by the Great Amen, "So be it." This great act of remembering proclaimed by the believing community and, indeed, the entire Church, both living and dead, affirms our faith that God has not forgotten us through the corridors of time but

Chapter Three: The Soul at Prayer

has fulfilled his promise that he would be with us always (Mt 28:20).

The Communion Rite begins after the Great Amen with the priest inviting the faithful to pray to the Father in the words that Jesus gave us. After the Our Father, the priest says some additional prayers for deliverance from evil and the gift of peace. The people then offer one another a Sign of Peace, an action which is followed by the Lamb of God and the breading of the bread. During this time, the consecrated hosts are distributed to the concelebrants present at Mass. The priest then genuflects and shows the consecrated bread and wine to the people saying, "Behold, the Lamb of God. Behold him who takes away the sins of the world. Blessed are those called to the supper of the Lamb." The faithful then respond, "Lord I am not worthy that you should enter under my roof, but only say the word and my soul shall be healed." The distribution of communion follows a process of the faithful to receive the body and blood of Christ distributed by the priests, assisting deacons, and, if necessary Eucharistic ministers. This process parallels the Offertory Procession in a unique way. While the latter represents the People of God presenting their gifts of bread and wine, the work of human hands to the Father, the former represents God's offering of the body and blood of his Son for the forgiveness of sins and the redemption of their souls. If the latter is a work of man, the former is a work of God made possible by the God-Man, Jesus Christ. The Communion Procession also represents the People of God's journey to the heavenly banquet, where they will be eternally fed by their loving Father, who treats them as his adopted sons and daughters. All during this time, our minds, hearts, memories, and imaginations are immersed in the miracle of faith that is taking place and filled with a spirit of thanksgiving for God's love for us. After Communion, we return to our places as the priest cleanses the sacred vessels. When he returns to his seat, the entire congregation rests in silence for what has just taken place. We lift our minds and hearts to God with deep, heartfelt thanks for the gift of Jesus' Body and Blood.

The closing prayer and dismissal come afterward. At this point, the entire Congregation stands and listens to the priest's final words as he blesses us, "In the name of the Father and the Son, and the Holy Spirit." Then he or the assisting deacon dismisses us, "The Mass is ended. Go in peace," to which we respond, "Thanks be to God." The priest and servers then reverence the altar, genuflect or bow before the tabernacle, and recess either down the main aisle to greet the people or directly to the sacristy. After Mass, we spend a few moments in quiet to absorb the full meaning of what has just occurred. We lift our hearts and minds to God in gratitude for what has just taken place, and we, too, join the recession as we leave the church and the priest to greet one another. Having received the nourishment of the Eucharist, we carry on with our lives bringing him with us wherever we go.

The Eucharistic Soul

As we have seen, God always acts as one, even though he is both one and many. We have also seen that, although he always acts as one, his creative, redemptive, and sanctifying activities are typically associated with one of the Divine Persons. Similarly, the human person always acts as one, by any one of our actions one of the four dimensions of our human makeup often comes to the fore.

Which of these dimensions will do so depends on the person's progress in the spiritual life. The farther along we are on the road to holiness, the more integrated each of these dimensions will be with one another. For this reason, when we gather for the Eucharist, we should not be too quick to judge which of the dimensions of our human makeup is operating at any particular time. For some, it may be only one; for others, it may be two or three; for still others, all four of these dimensions may be fully integrated in such a way. When we consider our belief that our Eucharistic worship is an action of the whole Mystical Body with Christ as its head, it follows that, regardless of which of these dimensions are prevalent in our own lives at any one time—the physical psychological, spiritual, or communal—all of them will be present in some way, because the whole Body of Christ is rendering praise and glory to God our Father. The Church is most herself whenever she gathers for and celebrates the Eucharist. As St. Irenaeus once remarked, "God's glory lies in seeing his sons and daughters fully alive with the vision of God" (*visio Dei*).[1]

When speaking about the Eucharistic Soul, therefore, we must be open to the possibility that, although our mind, heart, memory, and imagination may be

---

[1] Irenaeus of Lyons, *Against the Heresies*, 4.20.7.

prone to come to the fore at certain times of the Eucharistic celebration (especially during the Liturgy of the Word and when our memory and imagination are engaged during the Liturgy of the Eucharist), they may be fully engaged at *any* moment during the Liturgy. Indeed, to be fully engaged at all times of the Liturgy should be looked upon as the goal not only toward which the soul (*psyche*) must tend but also for which all the other dimensions of our human makeup must strive. For this reason, whenever we attend Mass, we should be intentional about involving our entire selves in the celebration.

Conclusion

We are multidimensional creatures, intrinsically one but with many facets. The soul (*psyche*) is but one of many dimensions in our human makeup. In this chapter, we have seen the various ways the celebration of the Eucharist engages it. We must remember, however, that the goal of our Eucharistic worship is to be fully present at all times on every level of our existence, even though we realize deep down inside that this is not always the case.

In present life, there will always be a gap between where the Lord wants us to be and where we presently are. The question we need to ask ourselves each day (and every time we enter the Church for Divine Worship) is whether the gap is getting larger or smaller. Because the soul itself has various dimensions (mind, heart, memory, imagination), we should reflect on the various ways in which we allow each of them into our celebration of the Eucharist. It is important because we are called to be intentional in our following of the Lord Jesus. Rather than just allowing the Mass to passively unfold before our eyes, we should seek to find ways to allow each facet of our soul (*psyche*) to be present at the Liturgy. In doing so, we will find ourselves narrowing the gap between vision and reality and able to worship God with all our heart, mind, soul, and strength.

The soul at Liturgy is in search of both God and self. It has come there embedded as a single facet of our human makeup to worship God in Spirit and Truth. It does so because God's grace has enlightened our minds, strengthened our wills, cleansed our memories and imaginations, and enabled us to see what takes place there through the eyes of faith is our only hope for becoming our deepest, truest selves.

Through these same eyes, it tells us that the Eucharist, as "the summit and source of the Christian Life,"[2] is a gift given to us as a means of living in friendship and communion with God and one day meeting him face to face.

Reflection Questions

- How are your heart and mind fed when you attend Mass?
- Do you listen intently to the Scripture readings?
- Does the homily educate your mind and touch your heart?
- Do you reflect on the readings and homily?
- Do you have a Eucharistic soul?

The Soul at Prayer

> Lord, I wish I could be constantly aware of your presence in my mind and heart. Help me to think and will all that you think and will. Help me place my feelings and emotions

---

[2] Second Vatican Council, *Lumen gentium*, no. 11.

under your vigilant care. I love you, Lord. Help me to love you more.

Chapter Four

The Spirit at Prayer

The Eucharist is also a time for the spirit (*pneuma*) to soar. Although this can happen at any point during the celebration, there are certain times when our spirits are more prone to prayer than others. In his First Letter to the Thessalonians, the Apostle Paul exhorts his readers thus: "Rejoice always, pray without ceasing, give thanks in all circumstances; for this is the will of God in Christ Jesus for you" (1 Thes 5:16-18). Since the Church is most herself when at Eucharist, it follows that our spirits should be most likely to pray in the fullest way possible during that time. Let us explore what it means for our spirits to pray.

Spiritual Breathing

Probably the best analogy we can use to understand how our spirits pray is the physical exercise of breathing. We are constantly taking in air and letting it out. We breathe during our waking hours and also when we are asleep. We would not be able to get through the day without this constant exercise of our lungs and diaphragm. Imagine trying to go about our daily business on a single breath. It would not be possible. Every journey we take requires the continuous in-and-out movement of our lungs. We breathe to take in oxygen from the air and breathe out toxic carbon dioxide.

The same holds for our spiritual journey. As with physical breathing, if we want to reach our journey's end, we need to "pray without ceasing." Unlike physical breathing, however, we cannot do this on our own. Prayer requires faith, which presupposes grace, which is itself a gift from God. Whenever we pray sincerely from the heart, God is helping us to do so. If we stopped praying, we would become lifeless inside, spiritually dead. What is more, much like breathing, we are not always conscious when our spirits are praying. It is so much a part of us that it moves to the periphery of our awareness. When seen in this light, our spirits are praying at every moment of the day, especially during the various parts of the Eucharistic celebration: the Entrance Procession, the Penitential Rite, the Liturgy of the Word, The Liturgy of the Eucharist, The Communion Rite, and the Dismissal.

Chapter Four: The Spirit at Prayer

Be that as it may, there are some moments during the Liturgy when our spirits come to the fore and shine. After the homily, for example, it is appropriate for the priest to return to the presider's chair and sit in silence for a few moments. Silence is the language of God. When we sit in silence as a believing community, we allow the Word of God that has just been proclaimed to penetrate our entire being as the Holy Spirit hovers over us and communes with our spirits. It is difficult to explain how this happens, for it cannot be measured or captured in words. St. Paul comes closest to describing it when he writes in his Letter to the Romans:

> Likewise the Spirit helps us in our weakness; for we do not know how to pray as we ought, but that very Spirit intercedes with sighs too deep for words. And God, who searches the heart, knows what the mind of the Spirit is, because the Spirit intercedes for the saints according to the will of God. (Rom 8:26-27)

During those few moments of quiet stillness, we breathe in the Spirit, and the Spirit sighs with our spirits and intercedes with the Father on our behalf.

The priest can also call for a brief period of silence at the end of the Prayer of the Faithful when the priest invites the faithful to add their intentions in the quiet of their hearts.

Another moment when our spirits come to the fore is after Communion when, having reposed the Blessed Sacrament and cleansed the sacred vessels, the priest returns to the presider's chair and sits for a few moments before the Prayer after Communion, the Final Blessings, and the Dismissal. These moments can extend a bit longer than the time after the homily. It's a time for rest after the congregation has been fed with the Body and Blood of our Lord and Savior. During this time the Spirit hovers over the entire congregation as we rest in our pews and yearn with the silent groans of the Spirit. After all, we are all "strangers in a foreign land." That is the meaning of the Greek word (*paroikia*) from which come our English words "parish" and "parochial." As the end of Mass draws near and as we return to our daily routines, we sense that we are mere sojourners passing through this life, beyond the pale of death and the boundaries of this present world. We understand that we have one foot in the City of Man and another in the City of God. We look forward to the day when we arrive at our true homeland in the place Our Lord Jesus has prepared for us.

The Silence of the Spirit

Silence has many facets and can be interpreted in different ways. It can convey boredom, as when a student in class doesn't listen to what the teacher is saying. It can express indifference, as when we give a blank stare to the person talking to us. It can give off a sense of coldness, and even hatred and disgust, as when we discount the person before us and refuse to give him or her the time of day. It can also communicate enjoyment and pleasure, as when we are immersed in an enthralling movie or book. Most of all, it can convey a sense of closeness and love, as when we walk beside a good friend and feel no need to say anything to him or her because our souls are one and there is no need for words.

Jesus once told his disciples that there is no greater love than to lay down one's life for one's friends (Jn 15:13) and that he no longer considered them servants but friends (Jn 15:13). Friendship (*philia*) is different from natural affection (what the Greeks called *storge*) as in the love of a parent for his or her children. It is also different from romantic love (*eros*) when two lovers stare into each other's eyes and are intoxicated with one another. It is also different (albeit related) from selfless love (*agape*), which is not preferential but given out equally to friend and foe alike.[1] As we have already seen, there are three marks of friendship: (1) benevolence and actively seeking the other's well-being; (2) reciprocity, so there is a two-way give and take among friends; and (3) a sense of mutual indwelling, so that we carry our friend's heart with us wherever we go.[2] In a certain sense, all four of these loves are one in God since the Scriptures use many images of parental affection, romantic love, selfless love, and friendship to describe God's relationship with us. We need only pray the Our Father and read the *Song of Songs*, the passion narrative, and John 15:13-15 to confirm this.

What is more, silence is involved in each of these loves. The quiet look of loving affection that a father

---

[1] For more on these loves, see C. S. Lewis, *The Four Loves* (San Diego: Harvest/HBJ, 1960).

[2] See Thomas Aquinas, *Summa theologiae*, II-II, q. 23, a. 1, resp.; q. 24, a. 11, resp.; Paul J. Wadell, *Friendship and the Moral Life* (Notre Dame, IN: University of Notre Dame Press, 1989), 130-41.

gives his young son as he tucks him in for the night; the silent stare of two lovers lost in their romantic embrace; the anonymous gift of self to someone in desperate need of help; the sense of belonging we feel when we encounter a good friend: each of these silences is different yet also similar since each of them expresses something beyond words, something words alone cannot convey. Silence is a complex reality, and we need to be able to sense its many nuances. We need to recognize the silence of the Spirit and the way it uses it to commune with us through his quiet embrace. In many ways, friendship represents the summit of all the other loves. The beauty of a father-son or mother-daughter relationship shines all the more once they become fast friends; when the romantic love between two people develops into a close friendship, their relationship deepens and remains solid, even after their romantic feelings for one another may dwindle over time; selfless love, as in the kind Jesus displayed when he died on the cross, becomes even more meaningful when that selfless love is transformed by his calling his disciples friends. The silence of the Spirit dwelling in our hearts reminds us that God made us capable of entering into a Holy

Communion with him and that is what going to Mass and celebrating Eucharist is all about.

The Befriending Spirit

The Holy Spirit is often associated with breath, wind, fire, a cloud, a dove, and many other symbols. At Jesus' baptism by John the Baptist in the Jordan, the Spirit descends on him in the form of a dove (Mt 3:16; Mk 1:10; Lk 3:22; Jn 1:32). In John's Gospel, Jesus appears to his disciples in the room where they were staying, wishes them peace, breathes on them, and says, "Receive the Holy Spirit. If you forgive the sins of any, they are forgiven them; if you retain the sins of any, they are retained" (Jn 20: 22-23). In the Acts of the Apostles, the Spirit descends upon in the upper room:

> And suddenly from heaven there came a sound like the rush of a violent wind, and it filled the entire house where they were sitting. Divided tongues, as of fire, appeared among them, and a tongue rested on each of them. All of them were filled with the Holy

Spirit and began to speak in other languages, as the Spirit gave them ability. (Acts 2:1-4)

The Spirit is a befriending Spirit. He is the source of unity of the Church who imparts grace to the Church and her members for the celebration of the sacraments and for living virtuously the gifts of "wisdom, understanding, counsel, knowledge, fortitude, piety, and fear of the Lord."[3] In addition to specific charisms, it also imparts the fruits of "charity, joy, peace, patience, kindness, goodness, generosity, gentleness, faithfulness, modesty, self-control, chastity."[4] These various gifts and fruits are God's way of helping us to live in communion with him. Good friends often exchange gifts with one another. The gift of the Holy Spirit is God's gift to us. We reciprocate by doing our best to live in the Spirit so that his numerous gifts and fruits may manifest themselves in us.

When he gave his disciples the gift of the Spirit, he commissioned them with the following words:

---

[3] *Catechism of the Catholic Church*, nos. 1831, 1845
[4] *Catechism of the Catholic Church*, no. 1832. See also Gal 5:22-23 (Vulgate).

> All authority in heaven and earth has been given to me. Go therefore and make disciples of all nations, baptizing them in the name of the Father and of the Son and the Holy Spirit, and teaching them to obey that I have commanded you. And remember, I am with you always, to the end of the age. (Mt 28: 18-20)

It is the Holy Spirit who propels the Church's missionary efforts. Without the grace that he imparts to us through the sacraments, gifts, fruits, and charisms, our efforts would all be in vain. When we cooperate with the Spirit, however, we partake in Jesus' missionary efforts down through the corridors of time. Jesus loves us so much that, through the Spirit, he allows us to share in his redeeming work. This is an honor that should not be taken lightly. Rather, it is a gift we should take seriously to heart, one that we should consider a sign of God's benevolent trust in his children.

Chapter Four: The Spirit at Prayer

Spirit and Eucharist

Since the Holy Spirit is the source of the Church's unity and the Eucharist is the "Sacrament of Unity," it follows that there is a close connection between the two. At the *epiclesis*, the priest, acting in the person of Christ (*in persona Christi*), asks God, on our behalf, to send down his Spirit upon our humble offerings of bread and wine. Similarly, after the Eucharistic Prayer, the priest raises the consecrated bread and wine and says, "Through him, with him and in him, O God, almighty Father, in the unity of the Holy Spirit, all honor and glory are yours forever and ever." To which the faithful respond, "Amen." In fact, as with all the sacraments, the entire Mass is prayed in and with the power of the Spirit. Without the Spirit, there would be no Church, no sacraments, no Eucharist, no gifts, no fruits, no charisms, and no missionary activity.

When we rest with the Spirit in the quiet of our hearts after we have been fed by God's Word and received Christ's body and blood, we do so in light of our call, the Church's call, to missionary discipleship. We celebrate the Eucharist to be fed on every level of our human makeup, and it is the Spirit who leads us on our missionary journey. At the end of Mass, when the priest dismisses the congregation, we are called to go out into the world to spread the Good News of our redemption through the passion, death, and resurrection of Jesus Christ. We do this not merely with words but especially by the way we live our lives. Jesus calls us to holiness: "Be perfect…as your heavenly Father is perfect" (Mt 5:48). We cannot love others, especially our enemies and foes, without God's help. The Holy Spirit is that help freely given to us out of the depths of God's mercy. He is our Comforter and Advocate. He empowers us to live holy and virtuous lives. Without him, we can do nothing. But with him "all things are possible" (Mt 19:26).

We do not leave the Spirit behind when the Mass is over, and we go our separate ways. We take him with us wherever we go, as we celebrate the Eucharist of our lives by offering ourselves in lives of service to others. The Spirit moves us to be instruments of change in a world that is in danger of being overwhelmed by the darkness in people's hearts. We are called to pray at all times and to ask the Spirit for the grace to step out of his way and let him gently take possession of our souls so that the world will be a better place in our little corner of the world. Each of us has a special calling from God. We must seek the Spirit's guidance so we can discover what it is and allow him to lead us in accomplishing it. Because of the Spirit, we can grow in holiness and bring faith, hope, and love to people's lives. We do this in the family, in school, in the workplace, in the marketplace, and wherever the Spirit leads us.

The Eucharist in Life

The Eucharist is food for our journey through Life and to the world beyond. It functions, however, in a very different way from normal food. Typically, the food we eat is digested and becomes a part of our flesh and blood. The Eucharist acts upon us in a very different way: we become a part of him. Jesus once said, "Very truly, I tell you, unless you eat the flesh of the Son of Man and drink his blood, you have no life in you" (Jn 6:53). He also said, "I am the way, and the truth, and the life. No one comes to the Father except through me" (Jn 14:6). The Eucharist is the sacrament of faith, the sacrament of hope, and the sacrament of love. It is the sacrament of sacraments and the sacrament of our salvation. When we receive it, we are incorporated more and more deeply into

Christ's Mystical Body. We are, in other words, in the process of becoming divinized. We are sharing in Christ's glorified humanity, so we can also share in his divinity. This was God's plan for us from the very beginning—to befriend us and accompany us throughout our lives.

Through the Eucharist, our reception of the other sacraments, and our lives of personal and corporate prayer, Jesus accompanies us by his Spirit throughout our lives. He walks before us to show us the way, behind us to catch us when we fall, beside us to accompany us on our journey, and within us to enjoy with us the intimacy of divine friendship. "God is love," we are told (1 Jn 4:16). The Father's way of allowing us to share in the intimate love of the Blessed Trinity—Father, Son, and Holy Spirit—was to send his Son to us in the person of Jesus Christ, who suffered and died for us to free us from our sins and overcome death. In Jesus, God did for us what we could not do for ourselves. He entered the darkness of the tomb and rolled back the stone on Easter morning to initiate a new phase in the history of humanity. He entered our world not only to redeem us but also to elevate us to a new state of existence. He came to initiate a new creation. As the Apostle Paul tells us:

> He is the image of the invisible God, the firstborn of all creation; for in him all things in heaven and on earth were created, things visible and invisible, whether thrones or dominions or rulers or powers—all things have been created through him and for him. He himself is before all things, and in him all things hold together. He is the head of the body, the church; he is the beginning, the firstborn from the dead, so that he might come to have first place in everything. For in him all the fullness of God was pleased to dwell, and through him, God was pleased to reconcile to himself all things, whether on earth or in heaven, by making peace through the blood of his cross. (Col 1:15-20)

By sharing in Jesus' glorified humanity, we also partake in his divinity, as well as his mission of transforming the old creation into the new.

We share in this mission by allowing the Holy Spirit to commune with our spirits, so he can empower us to live the Gospel and lead lives of holiness. As members of Christ's Mystical Body, our vocation in life (whatever it may be) is to bring his Gospel message to others. "Action flows from being," the saying goes. Christ's identity is intimately tied not only to his relationship with his Father in heaven but also to his redeeming and transforming mission. Moreover, he loves us so much that he wants us to accompany him in his task of transforming the world. He does this by befriending us, dwelling within us by the power of his Spirit, and moving us to act as he did so many years ago when he walked the Galilean countryside.

Conclusion

The spirit (*pneuma*) is not so much a part of the soul as it is a dimension of it that is open to the transcendent. To the extent that it is meant to spill over into and vivify the soul by entering into an intimate friendship with the Holy Spirit, we can say that it is to the soul what the soul is to the body. It is, so to speak, the "form" of the soul, something that redirects its end toward the divine. When seen in this light, the spirit seeks to flow into the soul and eventually spill over even into the body. We are called to become divinized persons, meaning that our friendship with Christ is meant to permeate every dimension of our human makeup.

Our spirits are most at home when we gather for the Eucharist. As we have seen, although they are present at each moment of the celebration, there are certain times when they move from the periphery to the forefront of our awareness. God speaks to us in silence, and we need to embrace those precious moments after the homily, at the end of the Prayer of the Faithful, or after the distribution of Communion when the entire congregation sits in silence to allow the Spirit to hover over it and commune with each of its member. For this reason, it is important that we not feel uncomfortable, even restless, in those moments of silence but embrace them as grace-filled opportunities to deepen our friendship with the Lord.

Once our celebration of the Eucharist has ended, our journey through Life continues. As members of a local parish, we are all "strangers in a foreign land." Having received the Body and Blood of Christ as our food for the journey, we find that Christ leaves with us and continues to bring the gifts and fruits of the Spirit to those we encounter. Christ has given us himself in the Holy Sacrifice of the Mass and seeks to live in us by the presence of his Spirit living in our hearts. His presence is not some symbol or mere metaphor, but a real presence. As members of his Mystical Body, we are called to befriend those around us and lead them to the one who has the words of eternal life (Jn 6:68).

Reflection Questions

- Do you ever sit in silence during Mass?
- Do you feel comfortable or uncomfortable when doing so?
- Does the priest allow for silence after the homily or after receiving Communion?
- Do you ever sit in quiet thanksgiving after Mass?
- Have you ever felt the presence of the Spirit at such times?

The Spirit at Prayer

Lord, bless me with a contemplative heart, so
I may befriend you in the quiet of my heart.
Help me to rest with you in the quiet of your

heart. Help me to understand the language of silence, so I can converse with you at all times and places. Help me to practice the presence of God since you are always present to me.

Chapter Five

The Community at Prayer

The celebration of the Eucharist is also a communal event. At such times the community of the faithful gathers to offer praise, glory, and thanksgiving to God as a single body. We do so as members of Christ's Mystical Body, a corporate reality that transcends the boundaries of time and space and spills over into the Eternal. Whenever we gather for Eucharist, we do so as the whole Church, living and dead: the Church militant, purgative, and triumphant. This communal dimension of the Eucharist comes before the individual worship we offer to God and highlights the social dimension of our human makeup. It seeks to reconstitute the corporate awareness humans shared before their original fall from grace and stands as an eschatological sign of the fullness of redemption we hope one day to share in its fullness.

Christ's Mystical Body

The Church is much more than the brick and mortar, stone and cement, of our fathering place for worship. The building itself is a symbol of a much larger reality. It represents more than even the community of the faithful who worship there on Sundays and weekdays. Although they represent the visible community of the faithful, they are but a small part of Christ's Mystical Body.

As St. Paul reminds us, "We walk by faith, not by sight" (2 Cor 5: 7). When we view the world through the eyes of faith, we see the world around us in a different light. The universe, we come to see, is a created reality imbued with both visible and invisible elements. What is more, it exists in the mind of God—as do we. According to our Catholic faith, we have immortal souls that are intimately tied to the material universe through our bodies. When we die, our souls are separated from our bodies but continue to exist. At the same time, they have not yet experienced the fullness of redemption since they are awaiting the resurrection of the dead and the reunion with their now glorified bodies at the end of time. At present, only Jesus' mother, the Blessed Virgin Mary, experiences this fullness since at the end of her earthly sojourn she was assumed body and soul to heaven and sits at the right hand of her Son as Queen of Heaven. Everyone else is awaiting the Second Coming of Jesus

Chapter Five: The Community at Prayer

when the dead shall rise, and their bodies be reunited with their souls, albeit in a transformed glorified way.

Given this understanding of immortality as found in the Nicene Creed, the *Catechism of the Catholic Church*, and other magisterial documents, our understanding of the Church must include not only the living but also those who have gone before us marked with the sign of faith. The disciples of Christ on this side of death are referred to as the Church militant, since we are engaged in life-and-death spiritual combat with the forces of evil that have infected our world as a result of humanity's fall from grace. Those who have undergone death but are not yet ready to see God face-to-face are called the Church purgative, since they still need to be purified and make reparations for their sins before they can enter the presence of God. Those who have experienced death and finally made their way into God's presence are known as the Church triumphant, since they have lived saintly lives and have been deemed ready to see God. When seen through the eyes of the faith, the Church embraces each of these states, all of which are present whenever we celebrate the Eucharist.

What is more, we also need to understand that while Christ's Mystical Body subsists in the Catholic Church, there are also various degrees of incorporation into it, depending on whether they are Churches, such as the Orthodox communions, that preserve priesthood and other sacraments, or other ecclesial communities do not maintain a valid priesthood and do not preserve all the sacraments. These various churches, ecclesial communities, and Christian denominations are incorporated in varying degrees into this Mystical Body. Even those who have not accepted the Gospel message and have embraced other non-Christian traditions, such as the Jews, Muslims, Hindus, and Buddhists, are oriented toward the Church in one way or another, as are all people of goodwill who seek to follow their conscience by doing good and avoiding evil. When seen in this light, the Mystical Body of Christ is a vast spiritual organism with Christ as its head and various members with varying degrees of incorporation and commitment to the truths of the Catholic faith.[1]

---

[1] Second Vatican Council, *Lumen gentium*, nos. 14-17.

Chapter Five: The Community at Prayer

The Church at Prayer

Because of the historical-yet-transcendental nature of Eucharistic worship, we need to open our minds and hearts to what is happening when we gather for Mass each Sunday. We need to be aware that what is going on is not a bunch of people gathered as individuals to bring our distinct needs to God (however true that might be on some level), but the prayer of Christ himself, who has incorporated his followers into on supernatural organism that has a collective awareness, while each member still retains his or her identity. When we gather for worship, in other words, we do so not as individual believers, but as a community, a collective entity, with a developing awareness that we belong to Christ, who lives in our minds and hearts and who, as such, transforms us from the inside-out by enlightening our minds, strengthening our wills, cleansing our memories and imaginations, and placing our unruly emotions under the gentle rule of reason's reign.

The Eucharist, in other words, is not merely an action of those gathered physically for worship, or even of those present in spirit by their varying degrees of incorporation into the Mystical Body, but of

Christ himself. At the height of the Eucharistic canon, the priest raises the consecrated bread and wine saying, "Through him, and with him and in him, O God, almighty Father, in the unity of the Holy Spirit, all glory and honor is yours, forever and ever." To which those gathered respond, "Amen." We worship the Father only in and with and through Christ Jesus, his Son. Jesus is the head of his Mystical Body, the Church. We can turn to God only because God himself has first turned to us through his Son, who entered our world, gave himself to us completely by his passion and death, and became nourishment for us by giving us his Body and Blood, and a source of hope for us in his resurrection and ascension to heaven. When seen in this light, our Eucharistic worship is intimately linked to Christ's relationship with the Father. As it says in the Gospel of John, "I am the way, and the truth, and the life. No one comes to the Father except through me" (Jn 14:6).

When we gather for the Eucharist, Christ himself gathers us as members of his body and allows us to be partakers in his glorified humanity. In doing so, he worships the Father through us, and with us, and in us, and, because of him, we worship the Father through him, and with him and in him. The Eucharist, in other words, is the means through which we have access to the Father. It is a theandric action, one involving both God and man. We have this access only because of Jesus' passion, death, resurrection, and ascension. And that was possible only because of the mystery of the Incarnation, where God entered our world and became one of us. Jesus was like us in all things but sin (Heb 4:15). Sin entered our world through Adam and Eve, our first parents, and was conquered through Jesus, the Second Adam, and Mary, our Mother, the Second Eve. Jesus is the firstborn of the New Creation (Col 1:15). Because of him, our present world is in the process of being transformed, and the Eucharist is the primary means by which this is taking place. It is the sacrament of the New Creation.

Attendants at Prayer

Given the above context of Christ's Mystical Body and the Church at prayer, we can now look at what the Eucharist means to those members of the Church militant who practice their faith on a day-by-day basis and who attend Sunday and often weekday Eucharist. In many ways, those physically present at the celebration are a microcosm of the whole Mystical Body and should incorporate into their collective worship a spirit of glory, praise, and thanksgiving for all that the Father has given them through the redeeming work of his Son. What does this mean concretely?

Above all, it means that we enter and leave our place of worship as a community of believers, seeking to be shaped in the way of the Lord Jesus. We know we live in a sinful world and that we have fallen time and again. We refuse to give up hope, however, because we believe that Jesus came not to call the righteous but sinners (Lk 5:32). Jesus loves us and believes in us. Through his death on the cross and his resurrection from the dead, we have been redeemed. Our sins have been forgiven and the way to the Father has been opened. All we need to do is believe in Jesus by denying ourselves, taking up our cross daily, and following him (Lk 9:23). To follow him is to walk in his footsteps in the way of love. We are therefore called to love God with our whole heart, mind, soul, and strength, and to love our neighbor as ourselves (Mt 22:37-40). This means keeping his commandments and placing the interests of others before our own (Jn 14:15). Most of all, it means walking humbly with

Jesus on his way to Golgotha. We must walk the way of the cross before we can rise with him in glory.

The Church is most herself when she celebrates the Eucharist. It is a time when all of God's people turn to him in prayer and profess their love for him. They do so as Christ's Mystical Body, all of whom are united to him as their head, and each of whom, as a member of his body, has a specific role to play in God's Providential plan for humanity and, yes, for all creation. It is the Spirit who, uniting us to Christ and to one another, enables us to be members of the whole while at the same time maintaining our unique identities. The Spirit, so to speak, takes possession of us, yet, at the same time, allows us to pursue truth and holiness and therefore become persons God envisions us to be. When we gather for Eucharist, the Sacrament of Sacraments, we pray to him as his adopted sons and daughters who, made in his image and likeness, render him, through Christ his Son, continuous honor and glory and praise.

Communal Oneness

When we view the celebration of the Eucharist as one that involves the whole Church (and not just those in attendance), the communal actions take on more significance. Our responses to the celebrant's words, for example, are not merely *our* response but that of the entire People of God. When we process to the front for Communion, we do so with all believers both living and dead. Our singing joins with that of the angels and saints. Our common gestures are joined with all the faithful. Our silent meditation joins us not only with God and one another but with those in purgative and the entire communion of saints in heaven. Because the Mass is both historical and transcendent, one involving both *Chronos* and *Kairos*, we touch the Eternal as the Eternal touches us.

The universal dimension of every Eucharistic celebration highlights the importance for those of us who are still on our earthly sojourn to attend Mass on Sundays and to receive Holy Communion. Doing so brings us into close, intimate contact with our beloved ones who have died and are either with the Lord or still finding their way to him. When seen in this light, the Mass is a window into eternity, an icon that allows us to look beyond the limitations of time and space and peer into the Beyond. Our deceased loved ones are not just memories but living beings

Chapter Five: The Community at Prayer

beloved by God who live in communion with us, just as we live in communion with the Lord and he with us. Receiving Holy Communion thus takes on an even deeper meaning. Receiving it celebrates the unity and oneness of the entire Mystical Body of Christ, both living and dead, the Church militant, triumphant, and triumphant.

What is more, this communal oneness with Christ's body, the Church, underscores the all-embracing nature of the process of divinization, in which all members of his body partake. If it is true that God became man so man might become divine, then this process of divinization involves *all* believers, both living and dead, although how far along the way each member is in the process will vary. In one way or another, all believers are making their way to God. Even those who have reached the beatific vision (*visio Dei*) will continue to journey into the infinite mystery of God. Our journey into the mystery of God never ends. It simply has different phases through which all are called to pass.

When we remember, moreover, that the Mystical Body of Christ possesses all the dimensions of our human makeup—the physical, psychological, spiritual, and communal—we soon discover that our actions at Mass that engage them involve not merely us as individuals or the community of believers physically present at Mass, but each member of the Mystical Body. Thus, when we bow or genuflect, sign ourselves, or sing praise to our Creator, when we respond to the words of the celebrant and receive the Body and Blood of our Lord, we do so not only as individuals but as the whole body of believers. With Christ as our head and his Spirit who unites us, our every action at Mass is a theandric action, one that involves both God and man. Because of the communal dimension of our lives, it embraces us as individuals but also our relationship with the entire body of believers. This process of divinization is gently shaping us so that we can share in Christ's glorified humanity and participate in his divinity. In doing so, we also begin to share in his human and divine consciousness and are given back that corporate consciousness that we lost as a result of humanity's original fall from grace.

Going Forth

At the end of our celebration of the Eucharist, we go forth not as individuals but as a community of believers, the one Mystical Body of Christ. As we leave the walls of the Church, we bless ourselves with holy water, remembering that we are the living stones of the assembly of the faithful. We do not go out into the world alone but with Christ and the entire body of believers, both living and dead. We go out to preach the Gospel not only with our words but also with our actions, by the way we live our lives.

We do so by listening to the Word of God as revealed to us in the Scripture and Tradition of the Church and as interpreted by the Church's magisterium. We do so also by listening to God's Word as it is imprinted in our hearts and then following our conscience. These two dimensions of God's providential guidance—natural law and divine revelation—help us to discern good from evil, and one good from another. They give us clarity in difficult circumstances and enable us to navigate the murky waters of life in today's world. They help us remember the words of Jesus that we are in the world but not of it (Jn 17:16).

The depth of a disciple's love for Christ is a function of the extent to which he or she performs the corporeal and spiritual acts of mercy. If Jesus is the face of the Father's mercy, then mercy should be primary in our lives. Jesus once said, "Truly I tell you, just as you did it to one of the least of these who are members of my family, you did it to me" (Mt 25:40). We are all members of Christ's family because we are all created in the image and likeness of God and have a fundamental dignity that can never be taken away from us. As such, we are called to treat all human beings with respect and extend a loving and merciful hand to them when we find them in need. The corporal acts of mercy are feeding the hungry, giving drink to the thirsty, clothing the naked, sheltering the homeless, visiting the sick, visiting the imprisoned, and burying the dead. The spiritual acts of mercy, in turn, are admonishing the sinner, instructing the ignorant, counseling the doubtful, comforting the sorrowful, bearing wrongs patiently, forgiving all injuries, and praying for the living and the dead. The attitudes behind such actions are the mark of those who have truly denied themselves, taken up their cross daily, and followed in Christ's footsteps.

Conclusion

The celebration of the Eucharist is an event that immerses us in Christ's Paschal mystery. It is an action of Christ as head of his Mystical Body, the Church, and occurs both in and out of time, in both *Chronos* (chronological time) and *Kairos* (sacred time). Those gathered for Mass are gathered with the entire host of Christ's followers, the Church militant, purgative, and triumphant. This gathering of the faithful has been or is being redeemed by Christ by his passion, death, and resurrection. They celebrate this salvific event and, with Christ as their head, gather to give glory, honor, and praise to their heavenly Father.

The fruit of the Eucharist is divinization. When we eat and drink of the body and blood of Christ, we share in his glorified humanity and through it also his transcendent divinity. The consecrated bread and wine are no longer bread and wine but the body, blood, soul, and divinity of Christ. When we consume them, they are digested but we become a part of them rather than they becoming a part of us. A transposition of a higher entity onto a lower takes place. When seen in this light, the Eucharistic celebration is the chosen means by which God enables us to share in the intimate Trinitarian life. "God became man, so man might become divine." God's love is self-diffusive. He wishes to share that love with others, and he created us for that very purpose.

As we are gradually transformed into divinized persons, we become more and more like Christ. As such we share in his consciousness and can cry out with the Apostle Paul, "It is no longer I who live, but it is Christ who lives in me" (Gal 2:20). This corporate consciousness embraces our minds and wills, our feelings and emotions, and will eventually have physical repercussions, ones that will overflow into a glorified, resurrected existence. The beauty of the Eucharist is rooted in the beauty of Christ himself and is something he wishes to share with us. We who have disfigured ourselves through sin are healed and glorified through this sacrament, "the source and summit of the Christian life."[2] Because of it, we can give thanks to our heavenly Father, who willed to make us his adopted sons and daughters so that we might journey into the eternal mystery of his Triune love.

---

[2] Second Vatican Council, *Lumen gentium*, no. 11.

Chapter Five: The Community at Prayer

Reflection Questions

- When you attend Mass, do you feel as though you belong to a community of believers?
- Do you believe that you are praying with the entire Church both living and dead?
- Do you have a sense of communal oneness when you celebrate the Eucharist?
- Do you believe you are an organic member of Christ's Mystical Body?
- When you go forth, do you believe Christ lives within you and has sent you forth to proclaim his Gospel message?

The Community at Prayer

Lord, help me to see you those around me: in my family, in my relatives, in my friends, in my neighbors, in my acquaintances, in the strangers I pass on the street. Help me to see your image in everyone around me, especially in those who worship with me, both the living and the dead, both those still making their way to you and those who are already with you.

Conclusion

Sacrament of the New Creation

When we gather for the Eucharist, we do so both as individuals and as a community. The latter consists not merely of those physically present but of the whole body of believers: the Church militant, purgative, and triumphant. Every human person is potentially a member of this body and is, in many ways, a microcosm of the whole. We are physical, psychological, spiritual, and communal beings—and so is Christ's Mystical Body.

We are called to turn our entire lives over to God, and prayer is a primary way of doing so. For this reason, we must try to find a rhythm in our prayer that engages every dimension of our human makeup. Because each of us is created in God's image and likeness, yet also unique in all the world, that rhythm will be similar yet also different for each of us. We need to find that particular rhythm that suits us, for that particular way is how each of us is called to give glory, honor, and praise to God. We should look at the way we pray and relate to God on each of these dimensions. We should also ask ourselves if we are neglecting any of them. In the end, the rhythm of our personal prayer lives should lead us to the Eucharist, where each of these dimensions is fostered in Christ's Mystical Body.

This Body is a macrocosm of the human person. That is to say that Christ's Church also has physical, psychological, spiritual, and communal dimensions, each of which is expressed when the whole of Christ's Mystical Body gathers for the Eucharist. It is for this reason that the Liturgy engages our senses through gestures, singing, incense, images, statuary, colorful vestments, and the like. It is also for this reason that our minds and hearts are nourished by reading from Scripture and homilies that seek to bring us to an inner conversion of mind and heart, that we sit in silence with each other and with the Lord to allow his Holy Spirit to hover over us as a community and fill us with his peace, and that we worship the Lord together, to remind us that we are members of a much wider community of those, both living and dead, who have taken up the cross of Christ and followed him to death and, in death, to the empty tomb.

God created this world and brought us into existence so he could befriend us and live within our hearts. For this reason, there is also an environmental

Conclusion: Sacrament of the New Creation

dimension to our human makeup. He created us not to exploit his creation but to be its wise and prudent stewards. The Eucharist is the sacrament of the New Creation. When we gather to celebrate, we do so with the hope that the transformation of the Old into the New is already taking place and that we, the followers of Christ, have been given a role to play in it. This transformation was made possible by Christ's incarnation, passion, death, resurrection, and ascension into heaven. We are so loved by him that he allows us to participate in this redeeming action. As members of his Mystical Body, we join Jesus in being the firstborn of this New Creation (Col 1:15). Each time we gather for Eucharist we sing the song of this New Creation, as we await and yearn for its consummation at the end of Time.

www.ingramcontent.com/pod-product-compliance
Lightning Source LLC
Chambersburg PA
CBHW060845050426
42453CB00008B/832